GEORGE & MARTHA
WASHINGTON

PRESIDENTS
and
FIRST LADIES

iBooks
Habent Sua Fata Libelli

Ruth Ashby

Please visit our web site at:
www.ibooksforyoungreaders.com
Manhanset House
POB 342
Dering Harbor, New York 11965

Library of Congress Cataloging-in-Publication Data
Ashby, Ruth.
George & Martha Washington / by Ruth Ashby.
p. cm — (Presidents and first ladies)
Includes bibliographical references and index.

1. Washington, George, 1732-1799—Juvenile literature. 2. Washington, Martha, 1731-1802—Juvenile literature. 3. Presidents—United States—Biography—Juvenile literature. 4. Presidents' spouses—United States—Biography—Juvenile literature. 5. Married people—United States—Biography—Juvenile literature. I. Title.

E312.66.A77 2004   973.4'1'092—dc22   [B]   2004041955

ISBN: 978-1-59687-657-6

Produced by Byron Preiss Visual Publications Inc.
Project Editor: Kelly Smith
Photo Researcher: Larry Schwartz
Designed by Four Lakes Colorgraphics Inc.

Photo Credits: AP/Wide World: 42 (bottom); Art Resource, NY: 4 (top); Burstein Collection/CORBIS: 42 (top); CORBIS: 8, 11, 13, 14, 22; Library of Congress: 6, 10, 15, 16, 17, 20, 23, 24, 25, 26, 27 (top and bottom), 28, 29, 30, 31, 32, 33, 35, 36, 40, 41; National Archives: 34; Courtesy of National Museum of American Illustration, Newport, RI, AmericanIllustration.org: 7 (bottom); National Portrait Gallery, Smithsonian Institute/Art Resource, NY: 4 (bottom); North Wind Picture Archives: 5, 7 (top), 12; Private Collection: 18, 38

August 2024

CONTENTS

Words that appear in the glossary are printed in
boldface type the first time they occur in the text.

▶ INTRODUCTION ★ ★ ★ ★ ★ ★ ★ ★ ★

In 1788, George Washington sent a note of congratulations to a French friend, the Marquis de Chastellux, on his recent marriage. "Now you [have caught] that terrible Contagion, domestic felicity," Washington joked, "which like the small pox or the plague, a man can have only once in his life: because it commonly lasts him . . . for his whole life time."

George knew all about "domestic felicity." He and Martha Washington were happily married for a total of forty years. Their relationship was based on mutual affection and great respect. He called her "Patsy"; she called him "Old Man," or "Papa."

President George Washington during his last year in office. Painting by Gilbert Stuart, 1796.

At 6 feet 3 inches (191 centimeters) tall, George towered over her small 5-foot (152-cm) frame. To get his attention, Martha would reach up and tug on his coat lapels. "General!" she would repeat urgently, until he listened. And then, likely as not, he would do as she said.

Today we revere George Washington as a hero who, by virtue of singular courage, determination, and integrity, oversaw the difficult birth of the United States of America. We tend to forget that, like most famous people, George owed his reputation to a combination of character and good luck. Martha was part of that good luck. Toward the end of Washington's life, a testy old veteran of the Revolutionary War decided to take the famous ex-president down a peg. "What would you have been," he snapped at Washington, "if you hadn't married the Widow Custis?"

Martha Washington later in life, by an anonymous artist, after a painting by Gilbert Stuart, 1796.

It is possible that without Martha's support, George Washington would never have had the opportunity to become the "father of his country."

A RISING STAR

George Washington was born on February 22, 1732, to Augustine "Gus" Washington and Mary Ball Washington of Bridges Creek, Virginia. Though Gus owned a tobacco plantation and as many as fifty slaves, he was not wealthy, and the Washington family did not belong to the Virginia aristocracy. George was his third son. Gus had two older boys, Lawrence and Augustine, from a previous marriage. When Gus died suddenly in 1743, the older sons inherited the bulk of their father's estate.

At age eleven, George was stranded without much money on a small farm with a difficult mother and four younger siblings. Mary was stern, demanding, and overbearing. One of George's cousins later remembered, "[of] his mother I was ten times more afraid than I ever was of my own parents." Mary never encouraged her promising son or praised him for his accomplishments. As an adult, he saw her as little as possible.

Young George Washington at home with his family. Engraving, nineteenth century.

George Washington copied out these "Rules of Civility and Decent Behavior in Company and Conversation" when he was about twelve years old. Rule number one reads, "Every Action done in Company, ought to be with Some Sign of Respect, to those that are Present."

Luckily for George, he was rescued by his oldest brother, Lawrence, who was an officer in the British military. Lawrence had named his home Mount Vernon, after his former naval commander and had married into the Fairfax family, one of the wealthiest, most powerful families in Virginia. George began to spend most of his time at Mount Vernon and at Belvoir, the plantation owned by the Fairfax family. Anxious to impress, he tried to imitate upper-class manners, even copying down phrases from an etiquette book: "Cleanse not your teeth with the tablecloth." "Kill not vermin in the sight of others." "Let your countenance be pleasant but in serious matters somewhat grave."

The earnest, gangly teenager became a Fairfax favorite, and George was soon good friends with young George William, the heir to the Fairfax estate. When Virginia's largest landowner, Thomas, Lord Fairfax, visited from England, George impressed him with his riding skills. Thomas Jefferson later described the adult Washington as "the best horseman of his age, and the most graceful figure that could be seen on horseback."

Young Surveyor

Despite George's obvious abilities, his future remained uncertain. How was he to make a living? The Fairfaxes offered to get him an appointment in the British navy, but at the last minute, George's mother said no. Lawrence then proposed that George become a land

George Washington's Real Birthday

George Washington was actually born on February 11, 1732—according to the "Old Style" Julian Calendar. In 1752, Great Britain and the colonies decided to adopt the "New Style" Gregorian Calendar. By adding eleven days, the Gregorian Calendar corrected errors and moved the start of the new year from March 25 to January 1. Thus Washington's birthday became February 22.

surveyor. As settlers moved west, surveyors were needed to map the wilderness and measure it out in farm-sized lots. As it happened, George was a math whiz and already owned a set of surveying instruments, left to him by his father.

Thus by the time George was fifteen, he was earning good money surveying the western Fairfax lands in Virginia. At first, as he admitted to his diary, he was "not so good a woodsman." Soon he learned to sleep on a bear skin before an open fire, to paddle upriver in a rainstorm, and to shoot wild turkeys and cook them on a forked stick. It was a great adventure for a teenage boy. His years in the woods also taught George the self-reliance and wilderness skills he would need in the future.

Young George Washington, left, surveying lands in western Virginia.

When he was not braving the elements, George was practicing his social skills. He learned how to dance, how to dress well, and how to flirt with girls. In the process, he suffered numerous rejections and wrote some dreadful, sentimental poetry:

> *Oh ye Gods, why should my poor resistless heart*
> *Stand to oppose thy might and power*
> *At last surrender to cupid's feathered dart*
> *And now lays bleeding every hour.*

George gained a new confidante when his old friend, George William Fairfax, married a lively girl named Sarah Cary (Sally). Pretty, dark-eyed Sally was eighteen, only two years older than George. They developed a friendly, bantering relationship that they sustained by writing letters during George's long absences.

Early Adventures

George Washington's boyhood ended in 1752 when his brother Lawrence died of tuberculosis. Lawrence's death

George Washington visits with the bewitching Sally Fairfax at Belvoir. Painting by Meade Schaeffer, 1931.

was a tragedy for George, who lost at once his substitute father and his best friend. He did obtain Lawrence's post in the Virginia **militia,** however, and eventually inherited Mount Vernon. At age twenty-one, George was suddenly Major Washington. If he impressed his superiors, he could earn himself a **commission** as an officer in the British army. Then his fortune, and his reputation, would be made.

Within a year, Washington volunteered for a delicate and dangerous British diplomatic mission. In 1753, the French and British were arguing over who would control the fertile Ohio River Valley to the west of the Appalachian Mountains (parts of present-day Ohio, Kentucky, West Virginia, and Western Pennsylvania). After the French built a chain of forts to bolster their claim, the British decided to threaten them with force. Washington was entrusted with a letter from Lieutenant Governor Robert Dinwiddie of Virginia demanding that the French withdraw—or else.

With six men, George set off across 500 miles (805 kilometers) of forest to find the French commander at Fort LeBoeuf, located in Pennsylvania. He delivered his letter and turned around to struggle back through the severe winter weather. After his horses collapsed, he continued on foot with a frontier scout. As they tried to cross the Allegheny River on a raft, Washington was thrown into the icy

George Washington and scout Christopher Gist crossing the icy Allegheny River on a log raft. Engraving, 1842, after a painting by Daniel Huntington.

water. "I fortunately saved myself by catching hold of one of the raft logs," he wrote in his journal.

The Journal of Major George Washington was published to acclaim in both the colonies and Great Britain upon Washington's return. He was promoted to lieutenant colonel and given the task of building a fort at the Forks of the Ohio, where the Allegheny and Monongahela Rivers join to form the Ohio River in Pennsylvania. His regiment surprised a French patrol and killed their commander. It was George's first experience of combat, and he was drawn to it. "I can assure you," he wrote his younger brother, Jack, "I heard Bullets whistle and believe me there was something charming in the sound."

The French claimed the French commander George's troops had killed was on a diplomatic mission. They accused the British of murder, and a diplomatic scandal erupted. Some scholars say that Washington's first military engagement was the spark that ignited a world war. Known as the **Seven Years' War** in Europe, and the French and Indian War in America, it eventually cost more than a million lives. Already, at age twenty-two, George Washington was making world history.

He returned home to a very annoyed Governor Dinwiddie and an entrancing Sally Fairfax, and promptly fell head over heels in love with his best friend's wife. It must have been a very painful experience. He was too honorable to try to seduce Sally away from her husband. All he could do was suffer in silence.

Fighting on the Frontier

Soon Washington had another opportunity to demonstrate his military talents. In February 1755, General Edward Braddock landed in Virginia with troops in tow. He had heard of the young Virginian's

The French and Indian War

In 1754, Great Britain and France were the most powerful nations on earth. Between 1754 and 1763, they were engaged in a long battle for supremacy in Europe, the Americas, and India. In North America, the French and Indian War ended in 1760 when British armies took the Canadian cities of Montreal and Quebec. Fighting continued in Europe until Britain and France signed the **Treaty of Paris (1763)**. Under its terms, France lost all its American colonies, except some islands in the West Indies. Canada and all the lands east of the Mississippi River became British.

expertise on the frontier. When Washington offered his services, Braddock promptly offered him a position as his **aide-de-camp.**

Washington quickly discovered that Braddock knew nothing about wilderness warfare. As the red-coated soldiers moved in close formation through the forest near Fort Duquesne in Pennsylvania, Washington warned that they were in grave danger of being ambushed. Then he fell ill with fever and **dysentery.** Barely recovered, he rejoined the troops only to hear the "unusual whooping and halloing" of attacking French soldiers and their Indian allies. The British troops panicked and ran. When colonial troops fighting alongside the British positioned themselves behind trees, the British shot them as deserters. Braddock himself was mortally wounded.

Washington tried valiantly to carry out Braddock's orders and rally the troops. As usual under fire, he was cool and fearless. He was also very fortunate. "I luckily escaped without a wound, though I had four bullets through my coat and two horses shot under me," he remembered later. When Braddock died, it was Washington who organized the retreat and guided the survivors back to safety. Of the 1,400 **redcoats** who set out, 950 were killed or wounded.

Braddock's defeat was a disaster for the British army, but it

General Edward Braddock is fatally shot, while Washington rallies the troops against French and Indian attacks. Painting by Junius Brutus Sterns, 1849–1856.

made George Washington an American hero. He also learned that the British army was not invincible. "The dastardly behavior of those they call regulars exposed all others that were inclined to do their duty to almost certain death," he wrote his mother in disgust. "They ran as sheep pursued by dogs."

The British abandoned Virginia and left to fight

the French along the Canadian frontier. It then fell to twenty-three-year-old George, named the commander in chief of all Virginia forces, to defend the western settlements. For three long years, Colonel Washington and his regiment tried to protect settlers against Indian attacks. Finally, when the French retreated from the Ohio Valley, George felt he could resign in good conscience.

By then, George realized that no matter how successful he was in the colonial militia, the regular British army would never grant him the commission he deserved. Perhaps it was time for him to retire to Mount Vernon and become the country gentleman he had always wanted to be. To support himself in style, however, he had to transform Mount Vernon from a small farm into a profitable estate.

For that, George Washington needed a wife—a wife with money.

The thirteen original British colonies as they looked at the time of George Washington's birth.

The Thirteen Colonies

In 1732, the year George Washington was born, thirteen English colonies stretched along the eastern coast of the North American continent. From north to south, they were: Massachusetts (including present-day Maine), New Hampshire, Rhode Island, Connecticut, New York, Pennsylvania, New Jersey, Delaware, Maryland, Virginia, North Carolina, South Carolina, and Georgia. Each colony was a separate governing body, with its own assembly, royal governor, and laws. Colonists thought of themselves not as Americans, but as New Yorkers, or Virginians, or Georgians.

The colonies were not independent, however. They were ruled from afar by the British parliament. They could trade only with Britain, and if Britain went to war, the colonies did, too. Even so, colonists were proud to be loyal subjects of the British king and grateful to enjoy the rights of Englishmen. In 1732, no one could have imagined that within forty-five years, the thirteen colonies would revolt against the mother country—and win.

CHAPTER TWO

COLONIAL GIRL

Martha Dandridge was born on June 2, 1731, at her father's plantation outside Williamsburg, Virginia. Chestnut Grove was a fairly small farm, only about 500 acres (202 hectares), on which John Dandridge grew tobacco. Although not wealthy, the family could afford imported furniture and clothes from England. Like most planters of that time, John had African slaves to work the fields and care for the house.

The young Martha Dandridge. Engraving after a painting by Alonso Chappel, mid-nineteenth century.

Martha and her siblings were probably educated by a tutor on the plantation's grounds. From her tutor, she would have learned reading, writing, and arithmetic. Although her spelling was always erratic, Martha was actually well educated for a girl in the 1700s. She also learned dancing and horseback riding, essential skills in colonial Virginia. An old family anecdote says that once Martha rode her horse up onto her uncle's porch—and playfully threatened to ride into the house as a joke.

Martha's most important teacher was her mother, Frances Dandridge, who taught her how to run a large household. The mistress of a plantation was responsible for the feeding, clothing, and health of everyone on it, from her own family to the slaves laboring in the fields. Under Frances's tutelage, Martha learned how to cook, sew, weave, look after pigs and chickens, raise vegetables, cure hams, brew beer, concoct home remedies, manage household slaves, and entertain company. The excellent management skills Martha displayed as an adult she acquired from her mother.

Martha was very fortunate to grow up in a happy, affectionate home, untouched by death or misfortune. As the eldest of nine, Martha was expected to look after her younger brothers and sisters. All her life, she loved babies and young children. Even in the White House, Martha surrounded herself with young people.

A Love Match

By the time Martha Dandridge was fifteen, she was a lively, pretty girl, at a petite 5 feet (152 cm) tall, with brown hair and bright hazel eyes. It was time for her to make her debut in society. Probably in the fall of 1746, she went with her parents to Williamsburg, at

(1) THE BRAFFERTON   (2) THE COLLEGE   (3) PRESIDENT'S HOUSE

(4) THE CAPITOL   (5) THE COLLEGE (REAR)   (6) THE PALACE

Views of eighteenth-century Williamsburg, Virginia, including the College of William and Mary (top, center) and the Governor's Palace (bottom, right), where Martha Dandridge probably attended the annual Birth Night Ball. Engraving, 1740.

that time Virginia's capital, where she attended a series of dances, tea parties, plays, and other social events. She may have attended the annual Birth Night Ball at the palace of the royal governor, held to celebrate the birthday of the British king, George II.

Martha caught the eye of a man who had known her all her life. Daniel Parke Custis, twenty-one years older than Martha, was from a wealthy and prominent family. It was a love match, and her family was quite pleased with her choice, but Daniel's father refused to give his consent. An eccentric and difficult man, John Custis insisted that Martha was a fortune hunter and threatened to disinherit his son. Apparently Martha made a "prudent speech" to Daniel's father that made him change his mind.

Martha and Daniel were married on May 15, 1750, and moved to White House, Daniel's plantation. Little more than a year later, their first son, Daniel, was born. Soon there were three other children: Frances, John (called Jacky), and Martha (called Patsy). It was a happy marriage, and Daniel was inclined to pamper his young wife. He ordered a gold watch from London for her. Above each number on the face of the watch was a gold letter, spelling out M.A.R.T.H.A.C.U.S.T.I.S.

On Her Own

Their happiness would not last, however. First, little Daniel died, followed three years later by Frances. The family was thrown into

Martha Custis at age twenty-six, shortly before she met George Washington. Painting by John Wollaston, 1757.

mourning. Then, most unexpectedly, Martha's husband, Daniel, died as well, probably of a heart attack, on July 8, 1757. At age twenty-six, Martha found herself a widow with two young children and a large estate to run. Suddenly she was the wealthiest woman in the colony, with 17,000 acres (6,880 ha) of prime tobacco land.

Martha Custis allowed herself to grieve but not for long. A month after Daniel's death, she took over the accounts, paid the bills, and collected debts. To the Custises' agents in London, Martha wrote that she now had "the Administration of his Estate & management of his Affairs of all sorts," and asked them to send her an accounting of the White House tobacco they had sold.

Martha Custis knew that she still required a manager for her estates and a guardian for her children, however. She needed a husband.

Plantation Life

Plantation homes such as Martha Dandridge's dotted the coastal plain, called the Tidewater, of the southern colonies. A plantation was merely a large farm, ranging in size from a few hundred to many thousands of acres. George Washington's patron, Lord Fairfax, owned 5 million acres (2 million ha) in northern and western Virginia. Planters grew mainly tobacco and some wheat in Virginia, Maryland, and North Carolina, and rice and indigo, which is used to make blue dye, in South Carolina and Georgia. Each plantation was like a miniature village, with a large "great house" surrounded by outbuildings: a kitchen, smokehouse, springhouse (where meat and dairy products were kept cool), washhouse, outhouse, tobacco-drying house, barn, stable, gardens, and slave quarters.

Most of the labor on plantations was performed by black slaves, considered property to be bought or sold at the master's whim. Slaves lived in miserable conditions, in one-room cabins with dirt floors and windows without glass. Sometimes they were allowed to keep a few chickens or a garden behind their cabins. For planters such as the Dandridges and the Washingtons, slaves were a necessity. They could not run and maintain their farms without unpaid labor. For most colonial plantation owners, owning slaves was just considered good business.

A NEW LIFE

No one knows just when or where Martha Custis met George Washington. Probably they were first acquainted in Williamsburg before she was widowed. Sometime in the spring of 1758, they saw each other again, possibly at a friend's home. After just two or three meetings, they became engaged. Seven months later, they were married.

The courtship of George Washington and Martha Custis. George probably met Jacky and Patsy, his future stepchildren, at this time. Engraving by John C. McRae, 1860.

What did they see in each other?

At age twenty-seven, George Washington was in peak physical shape, with the muscular grace of a natural athlete. At an impressive 6 feet 3 inches (191 cm) tall and about 225 pounds (102 kilograms), he towered over most people of his time. He had reddish-brown hair and a well-shaped head. "In conversation," an old Virginia friend said, "he looks you full in the face, is deliberate, deferential, and engaging. His demeanor [is] at all times composed and dignified." All his life, George Washington was immensely attractive to women. Martha Custis must have been smitten.

Martha was just eight months older than George. Her Virginia neighbors remembered her as "a small, plump, elegantly formed woman. Her eyes were dark and expressive of the most kindly good nature; her complexion fair; her features beautiful; and her whole face beamed with intelligence . . . she was fond of life, loved the society of her friends, always dressed with scrupulous regard for the best fashions of the day." No doubt George was attracted to Martha's inheritance, but he was also attracted to her.

Most important, George and Martha must have understood immediately that they could trust and respect each other. Martha

Washington and Slavery

It has often been remarked that even as George Washington fought for the liberty and rights of his white countrymen, he kept more than three hundred black people enslaved at Mount Vernon. George, who grew up with slaves who cooked and served his meals and polished his shoes, accepted slavery as a way of life. Like Martha and nearly all white people at the time, he thought that black people were naturally inferior to whites.

As George grew older, however, his views on slavery became more complex. On the one hand, he came to favor **abolition**, at least in private, and vowed never to sell another slave. He had come to despise "this kind of traffic in the human species." On the other hand, he needed slaves in order to run Mount Vernon and even tried to recapture a fugitive. George resolved his dilemma by freeing his Mount Vernon slaves after he died. Martha's own Custis slaves, passed down to her grandchildren, were not freed. As a result, many black families at Mount Vernon were split up after George's death.

George Washington directing the work at Mount Vernon. He speaks to the overseer while slaves toil in the fields and his step grandchildren, Nelly and Wash Custis, play nearby. Lithograph after a painting by Junius Brutus Stearns, 1851.

recognized that George would be a responsible manager of her estates and guardian of her children. He could tell that she would prove a lively, capable, and affectionate companion.

An Old and New Love

After ordering a wedding ring, George went back to the Virginia frontier for one last military campaign before he resigned. He wrote Martha a farewell note, signing it "your ever faithful and affectionate friend." In these last months before his wedding, he struggled to smother his old, illicit love for Sally Fairfax. On September 12, 1758, he sent a letter to Sally back home at Belvoir:

'Tis true, I profess myself a votary of Love—I acknowledge that a lady is in the case—and further I confess that this lady is known to you. Yes, Madam, as well as she is to one who is too sensible of her charms to deny the Power whose Influence he feels and must ever submit to. . . .

You have drawn me, dear madam, or rather I have drawn myself into an honest confession of a simple Fact. Misconstrue not my meaning; doubt it not nor expose it. The world has no business to know the object of my Love declared in this manner to you when I want to conceal it.

Although George does not say so directly, it is clear that the "object" of George's love is Sally herself. We do not know how Sally felt about George or what kind of relationship they had.

(Sally kept this letter all her life. It was found among her possessions when she died.) We do know that George mastered his feelings for her and that he and Martha always remained good friends with the Fairfaxes.

On January 6, 1759, George and Martha were married. It was Twelfth Night, or the twelfth day after Christmas, traditionally celebrated as a day of revelry.

The Marriage of Washington to Martha Custis. Painting by Junius Brutus Stearns, 1849. Stearns places the ceremony inside a church instead of in Martha's home, where the wedding probably took place.

Probably they were married at White House, Martha's home, before a large group of family and friends. Legend tells us that George wore a blue suit with a white satin waistcoat and gold buckles on his shoes. All his life he was an elegant dresser, aware of the social statement that clothes could make. Martha probably wore a gold brocade dress and purple satin slippers.

A month later, George, Martha, Jacky, and Patsy went to Williamsburg, where George took his seat in the House of Burgesses, colonial Virginia's legislative assembly. He had been elected in the summer of 1758, while he was still on the frontier. Then they left for George's estate at Mount Vernon. It would be George and Martha's home for the next forty years.

Mount Vernon Days

The couple settled quickly into a routine. As their livelihood was dependent upon the growing seasons, they kept what are called "country hours." George arose at four o'clock in the morning for a few hours of desk work in his study. He had to manage not only his own but also the Custis estate—five farms in all. Jacky and Patsy would each inherit one-third of the Custis estate, which George had to maintain until they came of age. The remaining third, bequeathed to Martha, became George's upon their marriage.

Martha rose at dawn and supervised the seven o'clock breakfast. Though George himself ate sparely of Indian (cornmeal) cakes and tea, the table was spread with a variety of fowls, ham, and game, as well as eggs, hot breads, molasses, and butter. There were always guests at Mount Vernon, both expected and unexpected, and the Washingtons seldom ate alone. It has been estimated that between 1768 and 1775, they entertained about 2,000 guests. One of Martha's tasks was to make sure that there was always enough food for whomever showed up.

Most of George's days were spent on horseback, inspecting his farm. His main crop was tobacco, Virginia's chief **cash crop**. When the tobacco crop was poor, he planted wheat, established fisheries, opened a whiskey distillery—anything to make money. Livestock had to be raised, fed, and slaughtered; buildings kept in repair; and fences built. In addition, Washington had to direct the overseers who managed the field slaves.

George played as hard as he worked. Never a puritan, he enjoyed his evenings in the local tavern, drinking, smoking clay pipes, and exchanging jokes. He loved fox hunting, horse racing, shooting, and, especially, the theater.

For her part, Martha supervised the household slaves at their work in the house, garden, kitchen, and other outbuildings. She was especially skilled at hanging and curing meat in the smokehouse. "Virginia ladies value themselves on the goodness of their bacon," Washington once wrote to his Revolutionary War friend the Marquis de Lafayette. Martha also oversaw the spinning and sewing of all the slaves' clothes. When the household slaves got sick, she treated them with medicines she kept stored in her bedroom.

Dancing was George's favorite diversion. He could dance until dawn—minuets and Virginia reels and fast country dances. When they were first married, Martha would dance, too, but she yielded the floor to younger women as she got older.

All his life, George loved to dance. In a painting depicting an imagined incident, General Washington dances the Virginia reel at a victory party held in 1781 after the Revolutionary War was won. Painting by Jean Leon Gerome Ferris, 1929.

Family Circle

Martha's favorite responsibility was Jacky and Patsy. She was a particularly indulgent and protective mother, having already lost two children to illness. Patsy was a frail child who unfortunately developed **epilepsy** as she entered her teenage years. Little was known about the disorder at the time, and the Washingtons were always searching for a cure. She was dosed with powders and "nervous drops," bled, and purged. Nothing worked.

Jacky was a lazy, good-natured boy who hated to study. He was mostly interested in "dogs, horses, and guns," as Washington complained to one of Jacky's frustrated tutors. George, who knew that one day his stepson would have to manage the vast Custis estate, was anxious to prepare him for a life of responsibility, but Jacky went his own carefree way.

Still, these were happy times. Both George and Martha found marriage very fulfilling, and they learned to love each other very much. Shortly after the wedding, George wrote a cousin: "I am now, I believe, fixed at this seat with an agreeable consort [wife] for life. And I hope to find more happiness in retirement than I ever experienced amidst the wide and bustling world."

Only one of Martha's letters to George survives. Written seven years after their marriage, it reflects the fond tone of their relationship.

March 30, 1767

My Dearest

It was with very great pleasure I see in your letter that you got safely down. We are all well at this time but it is still rainney and wett. I am sorry you will not be home so soon as I expected you. I had reather my sister [Anna Maria] woud not come up so son as May woud be much plasenter time than April. We wrote you last post as I have nothing new to tell you I must conclude myself

Your most Affectionate
Martha Washington

THE GATHERING STORM

While the Washingtons found peace at Mount Vernon, the world around them was in an uproar. Relations between the thirteen colonies and Great Britain were gradually deteriorating. The French and Indian War had left the British government in serious debt. In order to make the colonies bear some of the expense, the British parliament placed a tax on all printed material, including legal documents, newspapers, and playing cards. The Stamp Act, as it was called, outraged the colonists. This was taxation without representation! Their protests were so vociferous that the English repealed the law within a year.

Parliament was still intent on raising money. In 1767, it passed the Townshend Acts, which taxed imports such as glass, paper, and tea. Washington and others saw the acts as illegal and insufferable. He warned his neighbor George Mason in 1769: "At a time when our lordly masters in Great Britain will be satisfied with nothing less than the depreciation of American freedom . . . no man should scruple or hesitate a moment to use arms in defense of so valuable a blessing. . . . " Six years before the Revolutionary War began, Washington foresaw that Americans might someday have to fight for their rights.

A bird's-eye view of Mount Vernon, Virginia. Lithograph, mid-nineteenth century.

Colonists responded to the Townshend Acts by **boycotting** taxed goods and producing their own homemade products. In Virginia, Washington helped draw up a list of goods to be boycotted by the colony. Mount Vernon became a small factory where blacksmiths, spinners, and weavers made products such as homespun cloth and other goods. When the British removed taxes on everything but tea, things quieted down for a while.

An Unexpected Tragedy

Meanwhile, Martha's children were growing up. Just eighteen, Jacky Custis had fallen in love with a fifteen-year-old girl, Eleanor Calvert, and became engaged to her. George thought Jacky was much too young and immature to get married and made him promise to wait. Then he hustled his stepson off to Kings College (later Columbia) in New York City for a last chance at formal education.

He and Martha were even more concerned about Patsy. Her epileptic seizures had become more frequent as she got older, and Martha feared the worst. Then on a warm June afternoon in 1773, just after she rose from dinner, Patsy was "seized with one of her usual Fits, and expired in it, in less than two minutes without uttering a word, a groan or scarce a sign," as George told his brother-in-law Burnell Bassett. "This sudden, and unexpected blow, I scarce need add has almost reduced my poor Wife to the lowest ebb of Misery." Martha had been very close to her daughter. For the rest of her life, she would seek out daughter substitutes to love and to nurture.

Soon after, Jacky came home to comfort his mother. He married Eleanor, and they settled in Virginia to stay. It was a good thing Martha had her family close by in the coming years. Events were about to sweep them all into the maelstrom of war.

Colonists Fight Back

On December 16, 1773, colonists, disguised as Mohawk Indians, dumped tea from British ships into Boston Harbor to protest the remaining tax. The British responded harshly, shutting down the port of Boston and ordering citizens to house troops in their own homes. These "intolerable acts," Washington fumed, "exhibited an unexampled testimony of the most despotic system of tyranny that was ever practiced in a free government." The **First Continental Congress** was called to organize a unified colonial response, and George was chosen as a **delegate** from Virginia. When Washington and the other delegates left Mount Vernon for Philadelphia on

The Boston Tea Party, December 16, 1773. More than one hundred disguised men and boys destroyed 342 chests of tea while thousands of citizens watched. Lithograph, nineteenth century.

August 30, 1774, Martha Washington called out, "I hope you will all stand firm—I know George will."

When the Congress met in Philadelphia, they resolved to cut off trade with Britain completely unless Parliament repealed what became known as the **Intolerable Acts**. Washington went home to train the county militia. By the time the **Second Continental Congress** met the following May, fighting had broken out at Lexington and Concord in Massachusetts. This time, Washington purposely wore his old red and blue colonel's uniform to the sessions. If war erupted, he was ready.

Call to Leadership

Colonial troops had already gathered outside Boston to challenge the British army within the city. Massachusetts delegate John Adams realized that for the sake of unity, the Continental Army, the colonies' army, should be led by someone from a southern colony, preferably Virginia. He moved to nominate Washington as commander in chief. "I [have] in my mind for that important command," Adams said, "a gentleman whose skill and experience as an officer, whose independent fortune, great talents, and excellent universal character would command the [approval] of all America." So that others could speak freely about him, Washington slipped out a side door.

A few days later, George Washington formally accepted the appointment. In a humble, straightforward speech, he admitted his reservations: "I beg it be remembered by every gentleman in the room that I this day declare with the utmost sincerity I do not think myself equal to the command." However, he vowed, "[I will] exert every power I possess . . . for the support of the glorious cause." He refused to take a salary.

War had not been declared, and the **Declaration of Independence** was still a year away from being written. The fate of the American revolt rested upon George Washington alone. It took him three days to summon the courage to tell Martha what had happened. He knew how disturbed she would be. To Bassett, he wrote, "I am now embarked on a tempestuous ocean, from, whence, perhaps, no friendly harbor is to be found."

Just before George left for Boston on June 23, 1775, he scribbled a note to Martha: "I could not think of departing . . . without dropping you a line. I retain an unalterable affection for you which neither time nor distance can change. . . . Yr. Entire Go. Washington."

Then off he rode to join the colonial troops—and make history.

General George Washington. Engraving after a painting by Charles Willson Peale, 1787.

A Kind of Destiny

Only two letters from George to Martha Washington survive, both from June 1775. In this one, he breaks the news that he has been chosen as commander in chief.

June 18, 1775

My Dearest: I am now set down to write you on a subject which fills me with inexpressible concern. . . . It has been determined in Congress, that the whole Army raised for the defence of the American cause shall be put under my care, and that it is necessary for me to proceed immediately to Boston to take upon me the Command of it. You may believe me my dear Patcy . . . I have used every endeavour in my power to avoid it, not only from my unwillingness to part with you and the Family, but from a consciousness of its being a trust too great for my Capacity, and that I should enjoy more real happiness and felicity in one month with you, at home, than I have the most distant prospect of reaping abroad. . . . But, as it has been a kind of destiny that has thrown me upon this Service, I shall hope that my undertaking of it, is designed to answer some good purpose. . . . I shall . . . assure you that I am with the most unfeigned regard, My dear Patcy Yr Affecte Go. Washington.

CHAPTER FIVE

REVOLUTION!

Although George and Martha Washington experienced the Revolutionary War from different perspectives, they were both active participants. His task was to beat the British. Hers was to support her husband. He spent eight years on the move, living and fighting with the Continental Army. She also spent eight years on the move, in transit between Mount Vernon and the general's headquarters. Martha Washington, who until she was forty-four had never been farther north than Alexandria, Virginia, spent every winter between 1775 and 1783 in an army camp. She used to boast that she heard the last shots of one year's campaign and the first shots of the next.

George arrived outside Boston on July 2, 1775. By mid-November, Martha was packed and ready to join him. As she was now a public figure, her entourage was accompanied by a military escort for part of the way. In Philadelphia, she, Jacky, and Eleanor, Jacky's wife, were entertained by enthusiastic Patriots.

The almost triumphal journey north could hardly prepare Martha for the miserable conditions she encountered at the army camp at Cambridge, Massachusetts, just outside of Boston. George had been trying for months to bring order to the chaos, but the camp was still a squalid mess.

General Washington as he takes command of the Continental Army under an old oak tree, July 1775 in Cambridge, Massachusetts. Illustration, 1908.

Washington Takes Charge

Somehow General Washington had to whip fifteen thousand raw recruits into seasoned soldiers. Volunteers came from all the colonies: farmers from Pennsylvania, fishermen from Maine, frontiersmen

from western Virginia. They were undisciplined, disorganized, and distrustful of one another. "Connecticut wants no Massachusetts men in her corps," Washington wrote. "Massachusetts thinks there is no necessity for Rhode Island men to be introduced among them."

If anyone could unite them all, it was Washington. Cool, decisive, and superbly well-organized, he radiated strength and authority. He had to work hard to curb his explosive temper, though. Once, when a brawl broke out between the Massachusetts and Virginia regiments, Washington galloped off to break it up, sailing over fence rails. When he reached the crowd, he leaped from the saddle, lifted two soldiers up by their collars, and shook them. Roaring, he ordered the shocked troops to stop fighting.

General John Sullivan witnessed the amazing scene. "From the moment I saw Washington leap the bars at Cambridge," he wrote, "and realized his personal ascendancy over the turbulent tempers of his men in their moments of wildest excitement, I never faltered in the faith that we had the right man to lead the cause of American liberty."

Martha did everything she could to lighten her husband's burdens. With her usual knack for putting people at ease, she managed to get along with everyone. One New Englander, Mercy Otis Warren, described her first impressions of Mrs. Washington to her friend Abigail Adams, the wife of John Adams: "I think the complacency of her manners speaks at once of the benevolence of her heart, and her affability. Candor and gentleness qualify her to soften the hours of private life or to sweeten the cares of the Hero, and smooth the rugged paths of War." Martha Washington organized many social occasions for the officers and their wives, which helped relieve the strain of camp life.

Martha was there to see George win his first tactical victory over the British. His army was positioned on the hills above

A recruiting poster for General Washington's army promises soldiers an "annual and fully sufficient supply of good and handsome clothing, a daily allowance of a large and ample ration of provisions, together with sixty dollars a year in gold and silver money." In fact, Continental soldiers would suffer from shortages of food, clothing, and money throughout the war.

Boston, laying siege to the redcoats trapped in the city below. One night, under cover of darkness, crews dragged cannons up the heights overlooking the city. When British general Sir William Howe woke up the next morning and realized he was trapped, he offered not to burn the city in return for safe passage out of Boston. On March 17, 1776, Martha watched the British depart. The fleet sailed off to Halifax, Canada, where the British regrouped and planned their invasion of New York City.

The Rugged Path of War

Washington then led the Continental Army south to defend New York. Martha joined him, then went on to Philadelphia. Although the army built extensive fortifications in Brooklyn Heights and Manhattan, Washington knew his defenses were "but small and inconsiderable" when compared to the might and size of the British force. When 425 British ships arrived in New York Harbor on June 29, an American private declared in wonder that it looked as if "all London was afloat."

A few days later, the Continental Congress voted that the thirteen colonies were "free and independent states." On July 4, 1776, they signed the Declaration of Independence. It didn't help Washington in the field, however. On August 27, he lost the Battle of Long Island and was forced to retreat north of Manhattan. The British had captured New York.

Martha Washington remained in Philadelphia, not returning to

Benjamin Franklin, John Adams, and Thomas Jefferson all served on the committee to draft the Declaration of Independence. While the brilliant Thomas Jefferson was writing the first draft of the document, Washington was busy mustering his troops to fend off invading British troops in New York.

General Washington orders his men to retreat after the Battle of Long Island. A thick night fog hid the army's escape across the East River to Manhattan. Engraving, after a painting by M. A. Wageman.

Mount Vernon until the fall. There she immediately organized a mini-factory, directing sixteen of the slaves living at Mount Vernon to make cloth, shirts, and stockings to send to the Continental Army.

Washington, meanwhile, had been pursued by the British from New York into New Jersey and then into Pennsylvania. On Christmas night, 1776, he led his troops back across the icy Delaware River into New Jersey to surprise **Hessian** troops at Trenton. After this American victory, British general Lord Charles Cornwallis cornered the Americans at Trenton on January 2. Washington tricked Cornwallis by leaving campfires burning as a decoy while he sneaked behind British lines to attack Princeton, just miles away. In just nine days, General Washington had revived the American cause.

Washington retreated to winter quarters at Morristown, New Jersey, where Martha joined him in March. She brought wool and cloth with her from Mount Vernon and immediately organized local women into knitting and sewing circles. "Yesterday with several others I visited Lady Washington at headquarters," one Morristown woman later reported. "We had expected to find the wealthy wife of the great general elegantly dressed . . . but instead she was neatly attired in a plain brown habit. . . . We felt rebuked by the plainness of her apparel and her example of persistent industry."

George Washington crossing the Delaware River on Christmas night, 1776. Illustration, ca. 1912.

Washington's victories might have given him new hope, but he lost Philadelphia to General Howe in July 1777 and went on to suffer other defeats at Brandywine and Germantown, both in Pennsylvania. By the time the army moved into its winter quarters at Valley Forge, Pennsylvania, in December 1777, morale was at its lowest ebb. Only the American general Horatio Gates's victory over the British at Saratoga, New York, on October 17, left the Patriots with any hope at all.

A Bitter Winter

At Valley Forge, almost eleven thousand Continental soldiers suffered in the cold. Their clothes were ragged, their feet shoeless. "You might have tracked the army to Valley Forge by the blood of their feet," Washington wrote to Congress. He spent much of the winter begging Congress for food and provisions for his sick, starving men. Still, more than 2,500 died.

George Washington, after the Battle of Princeton. Painting by Charles Willson Peale, 1777.

When Martha Washington arrived in February 1778, she was greeted with cries of "God bless Lady Washington!" She had brought with her much-needed supplies: ham and herring, cornmeal, dried fruits, bandages, medicines, and sewing supplies. One woman recalled, "I never in my life knew a woman so busy from early morning until late at night as was Lady Washington, providing comforts for the sick soldiers . . . every few days she might be seen, with basket in hand, and with a single attendant, going among the huts seeking the keenest and most needy sufferers, and giving all the comforts to them in her power."

To Martha Washington, who was used to being responsible for large numbers of people, the army camp was a larger and more needy Mount Vernon. It was natural for her to organize other officers' wives into doing good works. She became very popular with the troops, who appreciated her "motherly care." One Valley Forge regiment called itself "Lady's Washington's Dragoons."

Hope and Despair

In spring, Washington heard wonderful news: The French had recognized American independence! Perhaps they would come to the aid of the struggling colonies. Still, the war dragged on. The British couldn't decisively beat the stubborn Patriots, but they were unwilling to give up and go home.

Washington visiting the sick and wounded at Valley Forge. Soldiers were housed in damp log cabins that offered little protection from the frigid weather. "Here all Confusion," a doctor wrote, "smoke and Cold, hunger and filthyness."

By 1780, the focus of the war had shifted to the South. To the dismay of the Americans, the British under General Cornwallis took the major port of Charleston, South Carolina, on May 12. "I have almost ceased to hope," Washington said when he heard the news. The Carolinas did not simply fall to the redcoats, however. Fierce **guerrilla** fighters from the swamps and backwoods made hit-and-run raids on the British, keeping them on the defensive. The Continental Army joined in the attacks. By March 1781, Cornwallis had lost a number of important battles.

Victory at Last

Discouraged, Cornwallis moved the army to Yorktown, Virginia, and in early August set up camp along the Chesapeake Bay. Washington seized his chance. He would trap the British by marching his army south to Yorktown, accompanied by the very welcome troops France has sent to the aid of the Continental Army. Meanwhile, the French fleet would sail into the Chesapeake and block British escape by sea.

On his way, Washington and his entourage stopped off at Mount Vernon. It had been six years since he had been home. He was greeted ecstatically by Martha, Jacky, Eleanor, and four

The British army surrenders at Yorktown. General Cornwallis sent a subordinate to offer his sword to American general Charles O'Hara, on horseback. Painting by John Trumbull, 1824.

grandchildren he had never even met. Jacky, excited by all the military bustle, decided to accompany his stepfather to Yorktown.

In the siege of Yorktown, the Americans and the French together bombarded Cornwallis into submission. He had no choice but to acknowledge defeat. On October 19, 1781, he surrendered his army. Claiming illness, Cornwallis sent his second-in-command in his place. Washington, not to be outdone, also dispatched his second-in-command. As the British regiments stacked their weapons in surrender, the British army band reportedly played "The World Turned Upside Down."

Back at Mount Vernon, Martha and Eleanor received word that the Americans were victorious—and that Jacky Custis was deathly ill. Unused to the hardships of army life, he had succumbed to "camp fever," now thought to be **typhus**. He died two weeks after the surrender. To console Eleanor as well as to help her, George agreed to informally adopt the two youngest Custis children, Eleanor Parke Custis—"Nelly"—and George Washington Parke Custis—"Wash."

For all intents and purposes, the Revolutionary War ended with the Battle of Yorktown, but it was not officially over until the **Treaty of Paris (1783)** was signed two years later. During that time, Martha continued to spend her summers at Mount Vernon and her winters with the troops. On December 19, 1783, Washington was finally free to hand in his resignation as commander in chief of the Continental Army. "Having now finished the work assigned me," he said at the closing ceremony, "I retire from the great theatre of action." Then he set off for Mount Vernon, where Martha and his family waited for him.

Finally, the Washingtons were home together.

General George Washington resigns his commission as commander in chief to Congress, which met during that time in Annapolis, Maryland. Painting by John Trumbull, 1824.

General Washington

When George Washington accepted the appointment as general and commander in chief of the Continental Army, he had not been in the army for seventeen years. In fact, the whole of his military experience had amounted to only five years. And he was facing the mightiest, best-equipped military machine on the face of the earth.

How would he beat the British? He would wear them down. Washington decisively won only three battles in the Revolutionary War: Trenton, Harlem Heights, and Yorktown. (Princeton and Monmouth were fought to a draw.) He tried to avoid fighting major battles, explaining to the Continental Congress that "Our side of the war should be defensive." It was his strategy to "avoid a general action" and "protract the war." The strategy worked.

FIRST FAMILY OF A NEW NATION

After the turmoil and strife of the war years, the Washingtons were thankful to retreat to their country seat. "I am getting into [tranquillity and rural amusements] as fast as I can," George wrote to George William Fairfax in England. "Let the world or the affairs of it go as they may." Being home was hardly relaxing, however. After eight years of neglect, Mount Vernon was desperately in need of repair. Like many southern planters, Washington was "land rich and cash poor." He badly wanted to make his farm profitable again.

Martha was happy to return to managing her household. She also had her hands full taking care of her family. In addition to little Nelly and Wash, she hosted her other grandchildren; Eleanor Custis and her new husband, Dr. David Stuart; and George's nephews and nieces. Martha was especially fond of sixteen-year-old Fanny Bassett, the daughter of her favorite sister, Anna Maria, who had died in 1778. Fanny helped Martha with the younger children. "My little family are all with me, and have been very well," Martha wrote contentedly to a friend.

The world would not leave the Washingtons alone, however. General Washington was the nation's first celebrity, and everyone wanted to meet him. Mount Vernon, he wrote a friend, was like a "well-resorted tavern, as scarcely any travelers who are going from

After the Revolutionary War, George and Martha Washington lived at Mount Vernon with Martha's two young grandchildren, Nelly and Wash Custis. Lithograph, 1889.

In 1784, General Washington bids farewell to the Marquis de Lafayette from the front porch at Mount Vernon. A young French noble, Lafayette fought with Washington during the Revolutionary War and became a trusted adviser.

north to south or south to north do not spend a day or two in it." There was always a "glass of wine and a bit of mutton" for anyone who stopped by. Martha was kept busy caring for the constant flow of visitors.

The People's Choice

His friends kept Washington abreast of the latest news. The new American government set up under the **Articles of Confederation** was not proving successful. Because most power had been left in the hands of the states, Congress could not collect taxes, regulate trade, or even pass laws without the states' consent. As a result, when the nation suffered a period of economic decline after the Revolution, the national government could do nothing about it. "No day was ever more clouded than the present," Washington wrote despairingly to a friend. "I predict the worst consequences from a half-starved, limping government, always moving upon crutches and tottering at every step." Clearly if the new nation was going to thrive, the articles had to be revised and a new government formed.

A Constitutional Convention was called for Philadelphia in May 1787. Its first order of business was to elect Washington as president of the convention. He spent the long, hot summer presiding as delegates debated what form the

The Constitutional Convention

In the summer of 1787, fifty-five delegates met behind closed doors in the Pennsylvania State House in Philadelphia to hammer out a new **constitution** for the new nation. The most serious disagreement concerned representation in the new **legislature.** The Virginia Plan, which favored large states, called for a two-house legislature with seats in both houses being awarded on the basis of population. The New Jersey Plan, which favored small states, called for a one-house legislature in which each state had just one vote. Finally, a compromise was worked out between the large and small states. The United States of America would have a two-house legislature, in which seats in the lower house (the House of Representatives) were awarded according to population, and every state in the upper house (the Senate) would have two seats. The plan was known as the Great Compromise.

The Signing of the Constitution, painted by Thomas P. Rossiter, ca. 1860–1870.

new government should take. Conscientious as always, he set an example by attending every session and always being on time.

He never participated in the debates, however, believing that the president should not publicly state his opinion. Instead, Washington exercised his influence in informal gatherings after hours. In such talks, he made it clear that under the new constitution, state interests should be subordinated to national concerns. On September 17, 1787, the new United States Constitution was signed and sent to the states for **ratification.** Washington went home again.

George would not be at Mount Vernon for long. It was apparent to all Americans that the man who had brought them victory in the Revolutionary War was the one who should lead the new country. On April 14, 1789, a messenger informed George Washington that the **electoral college** had unanimously elected him the first president of the United States. The electoral college is made up of people called electors nominated by the voters in each state. It meets every four years to choose the president and vice president. John Adams would be vice president. Washington didn't want the job and wasn't sure he could do it, but duty called, and as usual, he heeded its summons.

A Triumphant Journey

Two days later, Washington started on the journey to New York City, the first capital of the United States. "I go to the chair of government with feelings not unlike those of a culprit who is going to the place of his execution," he confessed to his old friend Henry Knox. He couldn't help being moved by the tumultuous reception he received en route, however. The way was lined with cheering crowds, booming cannons, and flower-covered arches. The celebration culminated in a magnificent regatta, or procession of ships, in New York Harbor.

George Washington is sworn in as the first president of the United States on April 30, 1789. The inauguration took place on the balcony of Federal Hall in New York City.

Martha Washington, who had stayed behind to make arrangements, did not see the **inauguration** on April 30. She was not happy about the move. "I am sorry to tell that the General has gone to New York," she grumbled to a nephew. "When or wheather he will ever come home again God only knows—I think it was much too late for him to go in to public life again, but it was not to be avoided." She, too, was met with thirteen-gun salutes and enthusiastic crowds on the road to New York. By the time they arrived, young Nelly and Wash were practically sick from excitement. Even Martha had to admit in a letter to Fanny, "I have the pleasure to tell you, that we had a very agreable journey."

President and Mrs. Washington

George and Martha both knew that their every move set a precedent. As Washington said, "I walk on untrodden ground." To begin with, there was the question of title. What should the president and his wife be called? John Adams favored "His Highness" and the "Presidentress." Others proposed "His Mightiness," or even "His Exalted High Mightiness." George insisted on the plainer "President of the United States and Mrs. Washington." (The term first lady was not used for another sixty years.)

Both were aware that it was up to them to set the presidential style. As official hostess, Martha Washington began holding Friday evening receptions called "Drawing Rooms," which men and women both attended. Abigail Adams, who sat next to her at these affairs, was impressed by Mrs. Washington. "She is plain in her dress but that plainness is the best of every article," she wrote her sister. "Her manners are modest and unassuming, dignified and feminine." The plainness was deliberate, as Martha wanted to appear both elegant and unpretentious. It was important to be formal, she knew. She wanted guests to take the president seriously. But she did not want Americans to accuse the Washingtons of being haughty or undemocratic.

Washington held his levees, or assemblies, for male gentlemen on Tuesday afternoons, asking only that visitors be "clean and polite." He dressed formally in a black velvet coat and ceremonial sword and bowed to each guest. The official Thursday dinners for government officials and foreign diplomats were so stiff that everyone usually ate in silence. At the end of the meal, Washington would lift his wineglass and toast each guest individually.

Being constantly in the public eye could be a strain, as Martha confessed to Fanny, who had married a nephew of George's and was managing Mount Vernon in Martha's absence. "I think I am more like a state prisoner than anything else," Martha wrote. "There is certain bounds set for me which I must not depart from."

Martha Washington, Nelly Custis, and Abigail Adams (on dais at left) greet visitors at an official reception. Engraving, after a painting by Daniel Huntington, 1861.

Martha's grandchildren, Nelly and Wash, were a constant joy. Looking after them allowed Martha to escape the pressures of her official duties. She and George took their grandchildren on carriage rides around the city on Sundays. Sometimes they went to a little theater where the audience would rise and applaud as the Washingtons settled into the presidential box.

Martha had to nurse her husband through two serious illnesses in these first years. In June 1787, he had to have a large tumor removed from his leg. The doctors dug it out without anesthetic. A year later, he came down with pneumonia and almost died. Martha ordered that straw be placed on the cobblestones on the street outside the house to soften the sound of carriage wheels. "You cannot conceive the public alarm," Thomas Jefferson wrote a friend. "It proves how much depends on his life."

A Model Chief Executive

Everyone knew it was up to Washington to make the new constitution work. As chief executive, he had to define the president's responsibilities and his relationships with the other branches of government. Just as he had done when he was commander in chief of the Continental Army, Washington saw to every administrative detail himself. He read all official papers, made every important decision, and made every government appointment. For his **cabinet,** he chose the smartest and most able men he knew: Alexander Hamilton for secretary of the treasury, Thomas Jefferson as secretary of state, Henry Knox as secretary of war, and Edmund Randolph as attorney general.

As chief executive, Washington was careful not to perform any of the duties of the legislature, as defined by the Constitution. Unlike more recent presidents, he thought it was unconstitutional for him to propose laws or use his powers to influence Congress. He did go to the Senate once, to present an Indian treaty, but when he had to sit through a long, boring debate, he vowed it would be the last time. Washington never attended a regular session of Congress again—and neither has any president since.

As his first term drew to a close, Washington made it clear he wanted to retire, but no one would let him. "This is the event at which I tremble," Jefferson wrote to him. "The confidence of the whole Union is centered in you." Just a few years into the life of the new government, there were already mounting differences between Thomas Jefferson and Alexander Hamilton, now the heads of the **Democratic-Republican** and **Federalist** Parties, respectively. A strong hand was needed to keep the country together. As always, duty came first, and Washington was persuaded to stay.

A Difficult Second Term

Washington's second term, which began in 1792 and was based in Philadelphia, brought the greatest crisis of George's presidency. In 1789, the French Revolution had deposed King Louis XVI, and France had erupted into civil war. Within a few years, the war had expanded into a European-wide conflict, and revolutionary France went to war against Great Britain, Spain, and Austria. The war

President Washington and his cabinet. Left to right: Washington, Secretary of War Henry Knox, Secretary of the Treasury Alexander Hamilton, Secretary of State Thomas Jefferson, and Attorney General Edmund Randolph. Lithograph by Currier & Ives, 1876.

divided both the nation and Washington's cabinet. Jefferson sided with France, the United States' old ally, insisting that it was the obligation of the United States to support the cause of revolution and liberty. Hamilton favored Britain and stability.

Washington understood that it was dangerous for the young, still weak nation to become involved in European affairs. In April 1793, he issued the **Neutrality Proclamation.**

Great Britain ignored American neutrality, however, and seized American ships and sailors. Even though Americans were outraged, Washington still wanted to avoid war with Great Britain, so he sent Chief Justice John Jay to England to work out a treaty. Britain agreed to pay damages for seized ships but did not guarantee the right of Americans to trade with the French.

Pro-French Democratic-Republicans were certain Washington had caved in to Britain and subjected him to a storm of abuse. Newspapers called him a "tyrant" and "Emperor George." Never in all his years in office had Washington been so vilified. Although he could probably have won reelection again, he decided that it was time to retire. Naturally, Martha was very pleased.

By not serving a third term, Washington set a precedent for every president until Franklin D. Roosevelt. Amazed that anyone would voluntarily give up power, Britain's King George III declared that Washington was "the greatest character of the age."

On February 22, 1797, thousands of people attended Washington's birthday party and retirement ball. Two weeks later, John Adams was sworn in as president.

Washington's Farewell Address

When he decided not to seek a third term of office, Washington composed his Farewell Address with the help of Alexander Hamilton. He never delivered the address before an actual audience. Instead, Washington made sure it reached as many people as possible by publishing it in a Philadelphia newspaper. It was reprinted throughout the country and the world.

In the address, Washington advised the nation to remain neutral in European affairs. "Observe good faith and justice toward all nations," he wrote. "Cultivate peace and harmony with all. . . . Nothing is more essential than that permanent, [habitual hatred] against particular nations and passionate attachments for others should be excluded."

He also warned against the "Spirit of Party." He had seen how disputes between Democratic-Republicans and Federalists had rocked his administration and divided the country. Party politics, he warned, "agitates the community with ill-founded jealousies and false alarms, kindles the animosity of one part against another, [and] foments occasionally riot and insurrection." All citizens and parts of the country, he said, should continually work toward "carefully guarding and preserving the Union as a whole."

CHAPTER SEVEN

UNDER THE VINE AND FIG TREE

In March 1797, Martha and George returned to Mount Vernon, hoping to find peace and quiet under what George called "the shades of my own Vine and Fig tree." They had grown old in the service of their country. Surely they had earned some rest after all their years of hard work.

The final year of Washington's life began happily, with the marriage of Nelly Custis to George's nephew, Lawrence Lewis, on her grandfather's sixty-seventh birthday. In July 1799, he wrote out his will, leaving to his "dearly beloved wife" Martha the use of his estate for the rest of her life. His nephews each received one of his

The Washington Family. From left to right: Wash Custis, George Washington, Nelly Custis, and Martha Washington. To the far right is Washington's manservant, Billy Lee, who was with him throughout the Revolutionary War. Washington freed Lee in his will. Painting by Edward Savage, ca. 1789–1798.

swords, to be used only in the "defense of their Country and its rights." After Martha's death, George's slaves were to be freed. He was the only one of the founding fathers to free his slaves.

On December 12, 1799, George spent the day riding around his farm in the pouring rain and sleet. When he got home, he did not change his wet clothes for dinner. Although he had a sore

Washington on His Deathbed. Painting by Junius Brutus Stearns, 1851.

throat the next day, in the afternoon he went outdoors to see to the removal of some trees. His secretary, Tobias Lear, suggested that he take something for his cold, but Washington refused. "Let it go as it came," he said.

Early in the morning of December 14, he awoke with a high fever. By the time he let Martha send for help, he could barely breathe. Four times during the day doctors bled him, removing more than half the blood in his body. Still, he got worse. Finally he told Lear, "I feel myself going. I thank you for your attentions, but I pray you to take no more trouble about me, but let me go off quietly. I cannot last long."

At ten o'clock that night, Washington took his own pulse. Twenty minutes later, he was dead.

From her seat at the foot of the bed, Martha asked calmly if he had gone. "Tis well," she said when Lear nodded. "All is now over. I shall soon follow him. I have no more trials to pass through."

George Washington was buried in a small ceremony at Mount Vernon. Martha never again entered the bedroom where he had died. Instead, she moved upstairs to a small attic chamber, where she spent much of her time. In expectation of her own death, she burned all the old letters between her husband and herself. After a lifetime in the public eye, she wanted their correspondence to remain private.

Martha Washington died on May 22, 1802, with Nelly by her side. An obituary in the *New England Pedium* read, "She was the worthy partner of the worthiest of men . . . they lived an honor and a pattern to their country, and are taken from us to receive the rewards—promised to the faithful and the just."

Today, Martha and George Washington rest side by side in the family vault at Mount Vernon.

Bust of George Washington by Jean Antoine Houdon, ca. 1786.

George Washington's Teeth

Washington suffered from excruciating dental trouble all his life. When he met Martha, he had already lost about five teeth. By the time he was elected president, he had only two left. They didn't last long. Dentists made him a series of dentures, from materials such as elephant ivory, and cow, elk, and human teeth (never wood). His final set were carved from hippopotamus ivory, with a gold palate and springs made of coiled gold wire. In portraits, Washington's mouth often looks tight and compressed. It took a lot of effort to keep the heavy dentures in place.

This set of Washington's dentures are made of human and cow teeth.

TIME LINE

1731	Martha Dandridge is born on June 2
1732	George Washington is born on February 22
1750	Martha Dandridge marries Daniel Parke Custis
1751	Daniel Custis is born
1753	Daniel Custis dies; Frances Custis is born
1754	French and Indian War begins; John (Jacky) Custis is born
1756	Martha (Patsy) Custis is born
1757	Frances Custis dies; Daniel Parke Custis Dies
1759	Martha Dandridge Custis marries George Washington on January 6
1763	Treaty of Paris (1763) ends French and Indian War
1773	Patsy Custis dies; Boston Tea Party takes place on December 16
1774	First Continental Congress meets in Philadelphia
1775	First shots of Revolutionary War fired at Lexington and Concord on April 19; Second Continental Congress meets in Philadelphia; George Washington named commander in chief of the Continental Army
1776	British driven out of Boston on March 17; Declaration of Independence signed on July 4; Battle of Long Island takes place on August 27; Battle of Trenton takes place on December 26
1777	Battle of Princeton, January 3; Battle of Brandywine, September 11; Battle of Germantown, October 4; General Gates wins the Battle of Saratoga, October 17; Continental Army goes into winter quarters at Valley Forge on December 18
1778	Martha joins George at Valley Forge in early February
1781	British surrender to Washington at Yorktown on October 19; Jacky Custis dies
1783	Treaty of Paris (1783) ends Revolutionary War
1787	Constitutional Convention held
1789	George Washington inaugurated president April 30 in New York City; Martha moves to New York City; French Revolution begins
1790	George and Martha Washington move to Philadelphia
1792	Washington is reelected president
1795	Jay's Treaty approved by Congress
1796	Washington issues his Farewell Address; John Adams is elected president
1799	George Washington dies on December 14
1802	Martha Washington dies on May 22

GLOSSARY

abolition—the act of outlawing slavery.

aide-de-camp—a military aide.

Articles of Confederation—first United States Constitution.

boycott—to be part of a group that refuses to have dealings with an organization or person to protest or force into acceptance.

cabinet—officials who head government departments and who also meet to advise the president.

cash crop—crops that are mostly grown to sell to others, not for use on the farm.

commission—a formal certificate of military rank and authority.

constitution—document that establishes the laws and structure of a government.

Declaration of Independence (1776)—document proclaiming the independence of the thirteen colonies from Great Britain.

delegate—representative to a convention or conference.

Democratic-Republicans—political party that supported strong state governments and favored aiding France.

dysentery—an infectious disease that causes severe diarrhea.

electoral college—group of people chosen from each state that gives the official votes for the President of the United States.

epilepsy—a disorder of the central nervous system that usually causes convulsions.

Federalists—political party that supported a strong central government and favored aiding Great Britain.

First Continental Congress (1774)—Gathering of colonial delegates in September 1774 to respond to the Intolerable Acts and to establish colonial militia.

guerrilla—related to using surprise, harassing tactics, not open warfare.

Hessians—German soldiers paid by the British to fight during the American Revolutionary War.

inauguration—ceremonial installation into office.

Intolerable Acts (1774)—harsh laws passed by the British Parliament in 1774 to punish colonists for the Boston Tea Party.

legislature—branch of government that makes laws.

militia—army of citizens who serve as soldiers (untrained) during emergencies.

Neutrality Proclamation (1793)—document stating that the United States would not favor either France or Great Britain in the European wars following the French Revolution.

ratification—act of approving formally.

redcoats—slang term for British soldiers.

Second Continental Congress (1775-1783)—assembly of colonial delegates that set up the Continental Army, wrote the Declaration of Independence, and directed the Revolutionary War.

Seven Years' War (1756-1763)—European war between Great Britain and France. In North America it was known as the French and Indian War.

Treaty of Paris (1763)—treaty that ended the French and Indian War, which also became known as the Seven Years' War.

Treaty of Paris (1783)—treaty that ended the Revolutionary War.

typhus—disease marked by high fever, rash, and delirium, and transmitted by body lice.

FURTHER INFORMATION

Further Reading

Chandra, Deborah, and Madeleine Comora. *George Washington's Teeth.* New York: Farrar, Straus and Giroux, 2003.

Collier, James Lincoln. *The George Washington You Never Knew.* (You Never Knew). New York: Children's Press, 2004.

Collins, Mary. *Mount Vernon.* New York: Children's Press, 1999.

Gormley, Beatrice. *First Ladies: Women Who Called the White House Home.* Madison, WI: Turtleback Books, 2004.

Marrin, Albert. *George Washington and the Founding of a Nation.* New York: Dutton Books, 2001.

Mayo, Edith P. (ed.) *The Smithsonian Book of the First Ladies: Their Lives, Times, and Issues.* New York: Henry Holt/ Smithsonian Institution, 1996.

McPherson, Stephanie Sammartino. *Martha Washington: First Lady.* (Historical American Biographies). Berkeley Heights, NJ: Enslow Publishing, 1998.

Murphy, Jim. *A Young Patriot: The American Revolution As Experienced by One Boy.* New York: Houghton Mifflin, 1998.

Peacock, Louise. *Crossing the Delaware: A History in Many Voices.* New York: Atheneum, 1998.

Rappaport, Doreen. *Victory or Death: Stories of the American Revolution.* New York: HarperCollins, 2003.

Simon, Charnan. *Martha Dandridge Custis Washington.* (Encyclopedia of First Ladies). New York: Children's Press, 2000.

Smolinski, Diane. *Battles of the French and Indian War.* (Americans at War). Chicago: Heinemann Library, 2003.

Stein, R. Conrad. *Valley Forge.* (Cornerstones of Freedom). New York: Children's Press, 1999.

FURTHER INFORMATION

Places to Visit

Colonial Williamsburg
I-64 (Exit 238)
Williamsburg, VA 23187
(757) 229-1000

George Washington Birthplace
National Monument
1732 Popes Creek Road
Washington's Birthplace, VA
22443-5115
(804) 224-1732

Mount Vernon
3200 Mount Vernon Memorial
Highway
Mount Vernon, VA 22121
(703) 780-2000

The National First Ladies' Library
Education and Research Center
205 Market Avenue South
Canton, OH 44702
(330) 452-0876

Smithsonian National Museum
of American History
14th St. and Constitution Ave. N.W.
Washington, D.C. 20013
(202) 633-1000

Valley Forge National Historical Park
N. Gulph Rd. (Exit 327)
Valley Forge, PA 19482
(610) 783-1077

Washington Monument
15th Street, N.W.
Washington, D.C. 20500
(202) 426-6841

Yorktown Battlefield
Colonial Parkway
Yorktown, VA 23690
(757) 898-2410

Web Sites

Colonial Williamsburg
www.history.org/

The First Ladies of the United States
of America
www.whitehouse.gov/history/
firstladies/

George Washington Birthplace
National Monument
www.nps.gov/gewa

Mount Vernon
www.mountvernon.org

The National First Ladies' Library
www.firstladies.org

Valley Forge National Historical Park
www.ushistory.org/valleyforge/kids/
index.html

The President's House in Philadelphia
www.ushistory.org/presidentshouse

INDEX

Page numbers in *italics* indicate maps and diagrams. Page numbers in **bold** indicate other illustrations

About the Author

Ruth Ashby has written many award-winning biographies and nonfiction books for children, including *Herstory*, *The Elizabethan Age*, and *Pteranodon: The Life Story of a Pterosaur*. She lives on Long Island with her husband, daughter, and dog, Nubby.

www.ingramcontent.com/pod-product-compliance
Lightning Source LLC
Chambersburg PA
CBHW060945100426
42813CB00016B/2867